Seeds of
PROSPERITY
for a Financial
REVOLUTION

DR. SONYA L. THOMPSON

©2019 Sonya L. Thompson, Minneola, FL

Published By: Sonya L Thompson

in Minneola FL.

Titles may be purchased in bulk for educational, business, fundraising, or sales promotional use. For information please email: sonya@ariseministriesintl.com

Unless otherwise indicated, all Scripture quotations in the New King James Version (NKJV) copyright © 1982 by Thomas Nelson Inc.

Seeds of Prosperity For A Financial Revolution

ISBN: 9781076697240

First Printing

Printed and bound in the United States of America

DEDICATION

I dedicate this writing to my amazing mother, Dorothy Walton. I am so thankful that the Lord has preserved you to see His goodness in the land of the living. I honor and bless you because the Lord used your womb to release me into the earth. Because of you, and through the inspiration of the Holy Spirit, I am able to write books to impact the nations and **WE** get to leave a legacy for generations to come. We are experiencing the greatest wealth transfer we have ever or will ever see again and we get to do it together! What an amazing God! I love you!

TABLE OF CONTENTS

INTRODUCTION

"*Wealth Transfer***,"** were the words the Holy Spirit exploded in my soul late one evening, as I was in the middle of a financial transaction. The entrance of these words instantly awakened me to the truth, the reality and the feasibility of what we have been heralds of for so many years — the ***Great Wealth Transfer!*** As a result of these two words, the Holy Spirit has allowed me no rest, until His heart's desire for His people has been documented in writing. Know this, God has set the stage for the greatest wealth transfer the body of Christ has ever experienced or may ever experience again; and it's happening right now! This is our moment. Interestingly enough, He has chosen to release this global mandate, this REVOLUTION, this REVIVAL, through His daughters. As we assembled together, for the very first **EVER** Apostolic Wealth Gathering in our region, at King of Glory Church in Clermont, FL, I realize through the Holy Spirit, that we are writing history, and spearheading the greatest financial revival the body of Christ has ever experienced! What an honor; what a privilege, to be counted worthy to carry this great call!

Miriam Webster defines a **REVOLUTION** as: sudden, radical, or complete change: a fundamental change in political organization, especially: the *overthrow* or *renunciation* of *one government or ruler and the substitution of another by the governed:* activity or movement designed to effect fundamental changes in the socioeconomic situation: *a fundamental change in the way of thinking about or visualizing something:* a change of paradigm.

You are about to step into a radical and complete change; an overthrowing of your current financial government; a fundamental change in your socioeconomic situation and a paradigm shift in your way of thinking, **if** you will embrace these seeds of prosperity. This God breathed manual, will overthrow your current financial regime and the King of Glory will take His seat in your economy. There will be such a paradigm shift, that a revolution will be the only outcome!

WHAT IS WRITTEN ON THE PAGES TO FOLLOW, IS FOR THE INTENSE PURPOSE OF

PLANTING SEEDS OF PROSPERITY, WHICH WILL INEVITABLY PROVOKE A FINANCIAL REVOLUTION! These are the very words the Holy Spirit spoke to me concerning this book. He said, *"You are going to start a financial revolution in the body of Christ."* As I write this strategic manual, I literally feel the stirring of the Holy Spirit. I sense Him brooding over these waters, to bring an explosion of light into your soul, concerning this great wealth transfer!

As Noah preached and proclaimed the impending natural flood, I have been commissioned by the Holy Spirit in this hour, to declare to you, and warn you of the impending economic FLOOD that is coming. But our great God is giving us time to get to an ark of safety! It's obvious that it's already raining, but I assure you, it's going to flood. Where we are headed economically, I want to tell you, money alone will not save you. It will equate to a mere lifesaver in the middle of a vast and endless ocean. Like the people in the time of Noah, who had never seen flood a day in their life, we are about to see something in the economy which has never been seen before; something we are very unfamiliar with. If God's people do not get to the ark of safety, they will be consumed by this next great economic deluge. Beloved, it's raining, but there's a flood coming, and no industry will go untouched!

Seeds of Prosperity for a Financial Revolution will give you the strategic details you need to get to the ark of safety. This revolution will usher you into the greatest financial revival of your time!

SEED #1

THE MYTH ABOUT MONEY

The title of this chapter alone should keep you from putting this book down, and cause an intense curiosity to arise within, which compels you to read it without interruption, from cover to cover. One thing I can promise you, is as you allow the Holy Spirit to reshape your thinking and value system concerning money, your financial life will change dramatically!

Kingdom thinking must always take us back to God's original idea, purpose, intent and plan for a thing. God is doing just that in this hour, through a Word that has not left me since late 2016; and it's the word foundations. We must get back to biblical foundations, if we in fact want to have godly influence, manifestation and dominion on the economic mountain. Regardless of how society has changed or shaped its view of money, God has not changed His. Regardless of how society defines wealth, that has absolutely no effect on God's opinion of the matter. According to **Malachi 3:6,** God never changes. His inability to change is amongst a list of things that God can't do. *"For I am the Lord, I do not change."*

In 2017 my spiritual family was set on the timeline of Dominion. As I began to dig deeper into the Word, everything began to scream kingdom. As much as I thought I knew the subject, the Holy Spirit took me on a journey that has further transformed my thinking and my life. I have come to a place where everything is viewed through the filter of kingdom. Several months ago, this thread continued to flow through and expand my understanding of the subject of wealth and money from a kingdom perspective. I must confess, even with all the revelation I have received in the area of money, up until April 2019, I also held onto the myth, that money heavily weighed on the scale of wealth, until the Holy Spirit overthrew my financial government!

Since money is spoken of a great deal in Scripture, is one of the world's key focuses and a necessity for trade in our society, I believe it's imperative for the body to view it in light of the kingdom and to have the same mind about it as our Father does. In our society, when we speak and think of wealth, the very FIRST thing that comes to the mind of most people is MONEY. We have been modeled, molded and conformed to equate wealth with money and the things we can purchase with it. Now, let's address what you've been waiting to hear about, the myth of money.

What exactly is a myth? Miriam Webster defines a myth as a **popular belief** or **tradition** that has grown up around something or someone; an unfounded or false notion. How does this relate to money? Let's look at the book of Genesis and a few other Scriptures to see what money is according to God's standard and His way of thinking. Standard is another word the Lord has highlighted for the body of Christ in this hour. In relation to this subject, it means God has established, by His authority the REAL standard of money, wealth and riches, as it relates to the financial economy of kingdom citizens.

> *Now a river went out of Eden to water the garden, and from there it parted and became four riverheads. The name of the first is Pishon; it is the one which skirts the whole land of Havilah, where there is gold.* **And the gold of that land is good. Bdellium and the onyx stone are there.** *The name of the second*

river is Gihon; it is the one which goes around the whole land of Cush.

Genesis 2:10-13

"The silver is Mine, and the gold is Mine," says the Lord of hosts (Haggai 2:8).

Now let's look at *Exodus 12:31-36*

Then he called for Moses and Aaron by night, and said, "Rise, go out from among my people, both you and the children of Israel. And go, serve the Lord as you have said. Also take your flocks and your herds, as you have said, and be gone; and bless me also." And the Egyptians urged the people, that they might send them out of the land in haste. For they said, "We shall all be dead." So the people took their dough before it was leavened, having their kneading bowls bound up in their clothes on their shoulders. Now the children of Israel had done according to the word of Moses, and they had asked from the Egyptians articles of silver, articles of gold, and clothing. And the Lord had given the people favor in the sight of the Egyptians, so that they granted them what they requested. Thus they plundered the Egyptians.

Before we move forward, please note, there are many more Scriptures to support what I am about to reveal to you. As we can clearly see from the references above, God does not reference paper currency of any sort, with money or wealth. During the Exodus, He did not have the children of Israel take Egyptian currency with them, nor does He reference ownership of any type of paper currency in the Scriptures above or any that follow. Why? Because He is NOT the creator of paper currency or this world's monetary system. On the contrary, He calls the **GOLD**, good; He calls the silver His. He created **gold, silver, precious gems, land, fine wool, flax and other commodities such as, oil, cattle, etc.!** These are the work of and creation of His hands. These are a few of the standards of wealth in which the Bible speaks of; none of which includes the various paper currencies of this world!

So, if the standard of wealth mentioned above are the things which belong to God and are what He deems as kingdom wealth; and if we are heirs and joint heirs through Christ, to everything in the kingdom, then where is our inheritance? Where is our money? Who has it? AND, what are we supposed to do with it when we get it? Please let me at least answer the first question for you; The wicked! That's who has their hands on OUR wealth, and they know it! If this is the case, and it is, what are we doing running after the world's standard of wealth instead of our kingdom wealth? We have believed the myth that paper currency is money and wealth. You may need to take a breather, like I had to. I know you have a myriad of thoughts exploding in your mind right now; It's because your government is being challenged! I was up for two nights processing this. But hang on because this is going to get a whole lot deeper.

As long as I've been a believer, I have heard the bold declarations of, "getting our stuff back!" We run the aisles of churches because we got a word that it's time to get our stuff back. But, if the truth is told, we don't even know what OUR stuff looks like, because we have been so busy chasing after the myth of money. No one will admit this is the case, but a quick survey of our lives and our conversations proves differently. A quick glimpse at the many tears shed over a lack of money causes me to believe this is the case. For the record, Money is **NOT** the stuff of the kingdom. Money is not part of your inheritance! God did not leave you any money in His will!

We quote this Scripture all the time:

A good man leaves an inheritance to his children's children, But the wealth of the sinner is stored up for the righteous (Proverbs 13:22).

Evidently the sinner is keen on what wealth is and has hidden the real thing from us. They have presented paper money in the place of our wealth. But God says, really, they have been holding or storing it up until the body of Christ — the righteous, comes to its senses and goes after the precious commodities which rightfully belong to us! My friend, it is NOT money. God did not create money, doesn't own it, nor does He back it. It's not a kingdom standard. That's why its value is fleeting. I shared this revelation with a business partner a few weeks ago, and he literally lost his mind! I don't know about you, but I don't want a myth! I want my money now! I have a birthright and I want the inheritance that accompanies it!

SEED #2

THE REAL PURPOSE
OF MONEY

What is money? Let's look at what the world's monetary system is supposed to be for the body of Christ and how God sees money in relation to His people. We are going to strip MONEY of all power, right here and right now! Listen to me carefully, money is a medium of exchange and a SEED for kingdom people. That's all it's supposed to be, but we have made it to be so much more. I mentioned this in one of my previous books, ***Break Out of Poverty Into Financial Abundance.*** Money is designed to be SEED to those in the kingdom and a SOURCE of supply to the sinner. If you read the entire ninth chapter of 2 Corinthians in context, you will quickly realize Paul was talking about money as seed. This chapter is directed to one who has a ministry and a grace of sowing upon them.

> *So let each one give as he purposes in his heart, not grudgingly or of necessity; for God loves a cheerful giver. And God is able to make all grace abound toward you, that you, always having all sufficiency in all things, may have an abundance for every good work. As it is written: "He has dispersed abroad, He has given to the poor; His righteousness endures forever." Now may He who supplies seed to the sower, and bread for food, supply and multiply the seed you have sown and increase the fruits of your righteousness.*
>
> *2 Corinthians 9:7-10*

He supplies, or as the King James version states, "ministereth," SEED to the sower. This means He is only furnishing seed – money seed, to a bonified SOWER. Like a doctor, a sower has been elevated to that occupation by reason of practice, proficiency and ability to follow instructions. It's quite apparent that He supplies and multiplies money seed to the sower, for the very purpose of making **another** exchange. Does He do this in order to continue increasing money? No, to increase your store of *money seed.* How we view money and its purpose makes all the difference in the world. When our mindset concerning money's purpose is directly aligned with the heart and mind of God, then we are ready for increase and will see the manifestation of this wealth transfer.

The overflow of this exchange of money seed allows us the incredible opportunity of sowing it into the lives/soil of others, which in turn increases the fruits of our righteousness, bringing glory to God! When money's purpose is known, the holder's goal is to ensure God gets the glory through every single transaction. I hear believers talk about money as a seed all the time, but the grip on it and the affection towards it, proves these are merely words and not the truth of the heart. Those who truly understand that money is merely seed will permit it to flow to and through them.

This process becomes perpetual if we continually pull seed out of the fruit, or monetary harvests received from sowing. Too many eat most, if not all their seed and then wait until there is an impending need before they sow again! This cycle has many in the body of Christ in a constant state of financial crisis of not enough or just enough. A sower is ALWAYS sowing in some shape form or fashion. I personally sow money seed almost daily, as directed by the Holy Spirit. As a result, there's a constant flow into and through my hands. However, the money seed harvest is not the end of the wealth cycle, it's just the beginning to a beautiful end!

Your seed has inherent in it the germ of the FUTURE plant. So, it's important for you to understand that your future and your generational wealth is locked up in your seed! We even see a glimpse of this in ***Hebrews 7:9.*** Notice I didn't say that MONEY is generational wealth; It's locked up in the seed. This means, if you are one who is limited in or reluctant in sowing under the **direction of the Holy Spirit**, you are blocking the generational wealth God has for your family! What would happen to you tomorrow if the government suddenly decided to make a change in our medium of exchange? How much would your money be worth then? Therefore, it's important for those in the body of Christ to break free from the hypnotic state we are in where money is concerned. Those who continually see money from a supply or wealth perspective will always be in financial need and will continually be on a quest to try to make something designed for sowing as a source of wealth. Surely, we can do a lot of things with money seed, but we always need to keep its real purpose before us otherwise, abuse will be the outcome. Let's look at Luke sixteen for a moment.

> **"And I say to you, make friends for yourselves by unrighteous mammon, that**

when you fail, they may receive you into an everlasting home. **He who is faithful in what is least is faithful also in much; and he who is unjust in what is least is unjust also in much. Therefore if you have not been faithful in the unrighteous mammon, who will commit to your trust the true riches? And if you have not been faithful in what is another man's, who will give you what is your own?** "No servant can serve two masters; for either he will hate the one and love the other, or else he will be loyal to the one and despise the other. You cannot serve God and mammon."

Luke 16:9-13

God calls the world's money "unrighteous mammon." Unrighteous mammon is riches personified; it is money deified. Money takes on godlike properties, influence and qualities in our lives when we do not have the proper perspective about money. He says, if you have not been faithful in your relationship with money seed, who is going to commit to your trust, true riches? **And if you have not been faithful in what is another man's, who will give you what is <u>your own?</u>** If you don't have the right relationship with or know the purpose of the world's money, as it relates to you, it will limit your ability to gather kingdom wealth. He is literally saying, "I can't give you ACCESS to your OWN inheritance, because you don't know how to handle something as simple as money seed!" It's the equivalent to holding items of value for our children until they are older/mature and know what to do with them; Otherwise it will be wasted and undervalued! God sees our inheritance in the same light. He is desperately trying to bring the body of Christ to a new level of **maturity** in this area and it must happen quickly!

Let me close out this chapter on a very clear note, just in case this hasn't really been planted in your soul: Money seed is a tool to *acquire* TRUE wealth and riches. It's a tool to accomplish righteous acts that bring glory to God, through us. Let this seed take root and begin to blossom within, because you're getting ready for the greatest wealth transfer in history!

SEED #3

GIVE ME BACK MY BIRTHRIGHT!

If you feel anything like I felt, you should have jumped up and hollered "Give me back my birthright!" In the book of Genesis, we read the account of Esau and how he despised his birthright. His brother Jacob had cooked stew and because he was weary, and devalued his inheritance, he made an exchange for what was convenient, temporary and valueless!

> *Now Jacob cooked a stew; and Esau came in from the field, and he was weary. And Esau said to Jacob, "Please feed me with that same red stew, for I am weary." Therefore his name was called Edom. But Jacob said, "Sell me your birthright as of this day." And Esau said, "Look, I am about to die; so what is this birthright to me?"*
>
> *Genesis 25:29-33*

You might be saying, "I would never turn over my birthright for a pot of stew!" I beg to differ! This is exactly what the body of Christ has done! Because we have permitted the world to conform our thinking in this area and define OUR wealth on their terms, we have been tricked into turning over our birthright. We have taken something that immediately satisfies our "hunger" and exchanged it for our generational wealth! The body of Christ has bought into the myth of money, and like Esau, we have given up our birthright for a pot of stew. We have sold our birthright for convenience. We have exchanged our Father's resources and our inheritance for what is of little to no value in God's eyes. We've settled for money seed as our inheritance. While I was meditating on this, the Holy Spirit reminded me of the Canaanite woman who went to Jesus for the healing of her demon possessed daughter.

> **But He answered her not a word.** *And His disciples came and urged Him, saying, "Send her away, for she cries out after us." But He answered and said, "I was not sent except to the lost sheep of the house of Israel." Then she came and worshiped Him, saying, "Lord, help me!" But He answered and said, "It is not good to take the children's bread and throw it*

to the little dogs." And she said, "Yes, Lord, yet even the little dogs eat the crumbs which fall from their masters' table."

Matthew 15:23-27

Financially we are seeing the converse of this Scripture. The King's kids are supposed to be at the table, but we are literally at their master's feet begging for the crumbs that fall from their table! As you are aware of by now, your birthright is not being transferred in money. As long as gold was connected to our money, God was in our financial system, and this nation prospered; but now that's not the case. He cannot give you an inheritance through a medium of exchange which He is not legally connected to! But He can get money seed into your hands so that you can redeem it for what belongs to Him— to you.

WHAT IS THIS BIRTHRIGHT TO ME?

We really have no idea of what to do with gold and silver and other gems. If you are like me, you have coins and have stored them up for years, not really knowing what you will do with them, other than pass them on to your children. We are like Esau who made this statement: ***"Look, I am about to die; so what is this birthright to me?"*** In other words, we say, "what am I supposed to do with gold, silver, jewels, etc.? I need to pay my bills, feed my children, pay my mortgage and live. That's not money! We don't use *that stuff* to make an exchange in our normal course of living. We use paper money!"

We have put money in a place which has caused us to devalue and despise our true birthright. Wealth and riches have often escaped God's people, because we haven't identified it on God's terms and level, until now. I can declare wealth and riches will be in my house all day and night, but it will continue to be a mere illusion if I don't know what I am looking for. If my understanding of this wealth transfer is different from the Lord's, then I will never attain to it.

This scenario reminds me of a Bugs Bunny cartoon I used to watch when I was a child. There was a segment where he was thirsting for water in the desert. He dragged himself along the desert floor until finally, when he thought there was water in sight he began to laugh uncontrollably. When he got to the place where he thought there was water, he realized it was just a mirage! I used to laugh every time I saw it, because bugs bunny was so sure he had finally found water, but he quickly realized his mind had played a trick on him! This is the case in the body of Christ; we have been fooled by the mirage of wealth and riches called paper money, but that is changing right now!

Mark chapter four gives spiritual insight to the childish example I just shared.

> *Now these are the ones sown among thorns; they are the ones who hear the word, and the cares of this world, the deceitfulness of riches, and the desires for other things entering in choke the word, and it becomes unfruitful.*
>
> *Mark 4:18-19*

The word deceitfulness is translated delusion. It is a false idea of or belief concerning a thing. One of the definitions in the Miriam Webster dictionary is: **A false idea or belief that is caused by mental illness.** This mental illness or wrong belief is what has choked out the Word in the area of biblical prosperity! My God! Only mental illness would cause one to give up their birthright for a mirage! Unknowingly, the body of Christ has been suffering mentally in this area, because all our lives we have been running after the mirage of paper money as wealth. Since paper money isn't backed by gold anymore, it has no real store of value. It has the value the government says it has and that can change at any time. When we put money back in its proper place, we will come out of the desert and grab ahold of our REAL birthright and inheritance once again! When we see wealth and riches like He sees it, then we can run the aisles and celebrate as the children of Israel did, because the Lord has turned our captivity! Our laughter will not mimic that of Bugs Bunny chasing the mirage, but it will be the laughter of the sons and daughters of God who have come into their real inheritance and birthright!

> **When the Lord brought back the captivity of Zion, We were like those who dream. Then our mouth was filled with laughter, And our tongue with singing. Then they said among the nations, "The Lord has done great things for them." The Lord has done great things for us, And we are glad.**
>
> **Psalm 126:1-3**

We are on the cusp of a financial awakening that will lead to the greatest financial revival the body of Christ has ever seen! Yes, I said **REVIVAL and I said FINANCIAL!** The body of Christ is coming alive in this area right now. We have been dead to our inheritance, but now I call you out of this tomb and command you to come forth and live, in the name of Jesus! The kingdom of God suffers violence and the violent will take back their inheritance by force. I decree and declare that the gates of Hell shall NOT prevail against this revelation and our exodus! This is our Kairos moment. The same way Israel was snatched out of the grips of Pharaoh, God has snatched His people out of the hand of this world system and escorted us into our promised land, the land flowing with milk and honey.

SEED #4

HOARDING OR GATHERING— KNOW THE DIFFERENCE!

One of the dangers of financial increase, I am speaking of money seed, is the mindset of hoarding. When one hoards, they store up and hide away for personal comfort, security and satisfaction. When one hoards, they bury their money seed in dead assets. Now I am all for saving and so is God, but we must avoid the proclivity to hoard up money and possessions. When there's an affection for money or things, hoarding happens. We have bought into the mindset of the world that things are proof of and a badge of prosperity. I have seen folks who looked like they had it all together and were one paycheck away from disaster, while driving and living in the finest!

Many people are driving, living in and wearing seed that can change someone's life and accomplish a greater good for the kingdom of God! Obviously, God wants His children to live good, dress good and drive good. He promises to ADD to our lives when we operate in the kingdom system, He has established for us. we must be very careful of where we place value in this hour. Where your heart is, that's where your treasure will be. Our value system cannot be the same as those in the world. We should NOT be running after stuff. As much as we say we are not, a quick survey often proves differently. A quick peek into many churches tells another story. People will begin running and climbing the walls at the hint of gaining the world's treasures. Let's look at the Lord's instruction to the body in the book of Matthew.

> **"Do not lay up for yourselves treasures on earth, where moth and rust destroy and where thieves break in and steal; but lay up for yourselves treasures in heaven, where neither moth nor rust destroys and where thieves do not break in and steal. For where your treasure is, there your heart will be also."**
>
> **Matthew 6:19-21**

What God is saying here is, don't waste your time hoarding up what the world calls wealth, but use your money seed to make kingdom advancements, as led by the Holy Spirit! Those things done with money seed for the kingdom are a store of treasure and true value. When we do this, He will **add** houses and cars, land, fine clothing and a whole lot more of the world's stuff, because our heart's posture is correct. So, when we don't go after or focus on things, God gathers it for us; because we are about His business! I am even concerned about the vision boards people create. Have you ever noticed they have mostly stuff on it? Again, I must stress, I am not in the least bit saying there's anything wrong with a beautiful home and nice things. I like nice things! What I am saying is, don't create your own vision. Find out what God has for you and align your faith and vision with that. Otherwise, you will find yourself running after and storing precious seed in dead places. That my friend is not the mark of a sower, or a good steward! James shows us what happens to those who don't know the difference between hoarding and gathering.

For the love of money is a root of all kinds of evil, for which some have strayed from the faith in their greediness, and pierced themselves through with many sorrows.

1 Timothy 6:10

Years ago, I remember a pastor giving a testimony of buying a private jet. He figured he should have one because he was traveling all over the world and his constituents had their own private jets. This move cost him dearly! After a few years, he had to sell the jet quickly to keep from going under financially. It was then that the Lord told him, He was only responsible for what was needed for his assignment.

Over and above our needs, it's very important to allow God who does exceedingly abundantly above all we can ask or think, to make the additions to our lives. If we hoard and lay up our own treasures, we will have the responsibility of taking care of them, not Him! In addition, if we really believe He will do exceedingly abundantly above.., then we should have no problem at all waiting on Him and allowing Him to birth His desires in our heart. People who get frustrated because they want more, are people who do not trust or believe in the goodness of their God. He is a God of timing for sure and you cannot rush Him. It's not the money seed or things He is really focused on; He is looking at the condition of our heart as it relates to things. Although, we can in fact bypass God and get all the things we want, but in the end, we will be left wanting. This is one of the areas where most people in the body of Christ find themselves. When they can't pay for something, God gets the blame, as if He was teaching them a lesson, when in fact they hoarded instead of letting Him gather it for them. God has promised me a home beyond my dreams, but I am content to wait for His timing. I am in no hurry because it's mine and it will be there waiting for me on my path of obedience. The Holy Spirit is the master of timing and if we wait for His Kairos moments, then we will see supernatural and unprecedented favor, in the same magnitude Israel experienced, as they stepped into their exodus. Anything you gather on your own will become very evident in the hour to come. God does not fund our hoarding, but He will fund everything He gathers and brings to us.

Let me solidify this with a Scripture I have alluded to, which is so often quoted but not quite taken to heart.

> **"Therefore, do not worry, saying, 'What shall we eat?' or 'What shall we drink?' or 'What shall we wear?' For after all these things the Gentiles seek. For your heavenly Father knows that you need all these things. But seek first the kingdom of God and His righteousness, and all these things shall be added to you. Therefore, do not worry**

about tomorrow, for tomorrow will worry about its own things. Sufficient for the day is its own trouble."

Matthew 6:31-34

He said the Gentiles — heathen, foreigners or those outside covenant, *SEEK* after the necessities of life? The word **seek** means to have an affinity towards, to worship, or desire. This means their main occupation is self-preservation, by accumulating things and taking care of their personal needs. On the contrary, believers have been given the instruction to SEEK after the kingdom. The same word and meaning is used, but the affection, direction and focus are in the right place. To seek the kingdom means to find out and inquire God's way of doing and being right. We must find out what His desires for us to do with our seed; What He desires to add to our lives and when. We must gain revelation and instruction through His principles and position ourselves accordingly. When we do this, God will add everything we need, along with what He desires for us to have. This is the difference between gathering and hoarding. Hoarding is done by the arm of the flesh, which is what the world is doing, but gathering is a divine movement of the hand of God. He literally brings things to you or positions you in a spot to gather what He wants you to have. You will either work the garden to bring forth fruit, or just reach out your hand of faith and take it!

THE BLESSING IN GATHERING

The blessing of the Lord makes one rich, And He adds no sorrow with it (Proverbs 10:22). The blessing of the Lord empowers us and is a force that adds to us; but sorrow is an ever-present aspect of toiling. The blessing is the replacement for toiling, which is the world's portion. The blessing puts you back in the garden of Eden, where you till the ground like a son of God, but toiling keeps you out of the garden and causes you to work by the sweat of your brow. That's all the world system can offer you!

We can see this principle of gathering in the book of Genesis, when God gathered the animals to the ark. Noah was about God's business, warning the people and building the ark according to God's specifications

Of clean animals, of animals that are unclean, of birds, and of everything that creeps on the earth, two by two they went into the ark to Noah, male and female, as God had commanded Noah. On the very

41

same day Noah and Noah's sons, Shem, Ham, and Japheth, and Noah's wife and the three wives of his sons with them, entered the ark— they and every beast after its kind, all cattle after their kind, every creeping thing that creeps on the earth after its kind, and every bird after its kind, every bird of every sort. And they went into the ark to Noah, two by two, of all flesh in which is the breath of life. So those that entered, male and female of all flesh, went in as God had commanded him; and the Lord shut him in.

Genesis 6:8-16

During Noah's process of preparation for the flood, God gathered for him. He does the sending; we just provide the "ark" to take it/them in. Because Noah was in position for the gathering, God sent the animals to him. The Scripture states twice, that the animals went UNTO Noah. God sent them while He was working. Do you see how this mirrors **Matthew 6:33**? Let's work on the ark and let Him do the gathering, while the world is out trying to hoard, wearing themselves out for the finer things in life. We have a GUARANTEE of the best things in life when we walk with and obey God. When Noah finished the work and all the animals were secure as God had commanded, the Bible says, **"and the LORD shut him in."** Now, all that Noah had gathered from the hand of God was safe. God wanted to ensure they came out of the flood intact and with their wealth. Why is this considered wealth? Because every animal carried within him, the seed to reproduce. Seed is the key to generational and perpetual wealth!

This is exactly what our Father is doing with us in this hour. He is looking for Noahs who will be heralds about the impending flood and warn the people to get to an ark of safety! God is gathering for us and gathering us to a place of safety, because a flood is coming! If we posture ourselves like those in Noah's day who did not believe and continue going on about the normal course of things, we will be swept away in this impending economic flood! It's time to gather; This is not the time to take your money seed to buy stuff, unless God has given that instruction. After our gathering is done, He will begin to unveil a strategic purpose and plan for our acquired inheritance.

SEED #5
GATHERING WITH A PURPOSE

When the Israelites broke free from the Egyptians, the Bible says the LORD gave them favor—grace in the sight of the Egyptians and they plundered them! I hope you realize favor isn't just God being extra nice to you. Favor has a power behind it and in it. God's favor compels or puts pressure on those who are holding His stuff to turn it over to the rightful heirs! Oh! favor is fair! I think it would be unfair if the sons of God did not have access to favor. Surely, we are supposed to have this advantage as heirs and joint heirs of Christ. Favor is part of our benefits package!

As you have heard, undoubtedly many times, "If you don't know the use of a thing, abuse is inevitable!" I don't know who coined that phrase, but it is one hundred percent accurate on every single level. The same applies to this great wealth transfer that is presently occurring in the body of Christ. If we do not know, by revelation of the Holy Spirit, the purpose of our gathering, abuse is inevitable! One of the most eye-opening revelations of gathering with purpose gone wrong is found in the book of Exodus.

> **Now the children of Israel had done according to the word of Moses, and they had asked from the Egyptians articles of silver, articles of gold, and clothing. And the Lord had given the people favor in the sight of the Egyptians, so that they granted them what they requested. Thus they plundered the Egyptians.**
>
> **Exodus 12:35-36**

After four hundred years of bondage and here they were walking out with the wealth of the nation of Egypt! They had been crying out to Jehovah and He heard their cry and sent them a deliverer. The Israelites had absolutely no idea what was going to be required with what they were carrying out of the land. The passage below is a prime example of the inevitable abuse when purpose is not known.

Now when the people saw that Moses delayed coming down from the mountain, the people gathered together to Aaron, and said to him, "Come, make us gods that shall go before us; for as for this Moses, the man who brought us up out of the land of Egypt, we do not know what has become of him." And Aaron said to them, "Break off the golden earrings which are in the ears of your wives, your sons, and your daughters, and bring them to me." So all the people broke off the golden earrings which were in their ears and brought them to Aaron. And he received the gold from their hand, and he fashioned it with an engraving tool, and made a molded calf. Then they said, "This is your god, O Israel, that brought you out of the land of Egypt!" So when Aaron saw it, he built an altar before it. And Aaron made a proclamation and said, "Tomorrow is a feast to the Lord." Then they rose early on the next day, offered burnt offerings, and brought peace offerings; and the people sat down to eat and drink, and rose up to play.

Exodus 32:1-5

This is exactly what will happen in the body of Christ if we do not wait on the Holy Spirit to give an assignment for what we are gathering. We will build an altar to the stuff we have gathered and find ourselves right back in captivity again. We will be just like the Israelites who rose up to play with what was transferred into their hands! The body of Christ tends to misappropriate a move of God. When the Lord starts moving money seed into our hands, many in the church body will begin to bury it in depreciating assets. I learned many years ago, that when God starts to overload you financially, it is in **preparation** for what is to come. He is trying to protect you! Unfortunately, what many will end up with when "Moses" comes down from the mountain, is an idol. They will be content with their calf until God calls them on the carpet and unveils His purpose. If this mindset prevails, when this Kairos moment of gathering is over, many will have literally turned their money seed back over to the world, instead of making the necessary exchange.

This time of gathering can easily become a point of idolatry. He doesn't want you to get caught up in the commotion, so allow Him to catch you out of this system and into your wealthy place. Your **EXODUS** is here! What you have prayed about, cried about, decreed and declared and prophesied about is here! What will you do with this moment? What will you do with this revelation? What you do with your seed will determine your outcome in the years of famine. God has given us time to gather. How much time, you ask? **We have a three-year window which began approximately the thirteenth of June 2019.** We will continue to see the writing on the wall as we move closer to the closeout of this Kairos moment. I don't know about you, but I don't want to wait for another opportunity. I want my money now! I want my inheritance now! I will have my wealth transfer now! What about you?

This passage also gives light into the purpose of gathering.

Then the Lord spoke to Moses, saying: "Speak to the children of Israel, that they bring Me an offering. From everyone who gives it willingly with his heart you shall take My offering. And this is the offering which you shall take from them: gold, silver, and bronze; blue, purple, and scarlet thread, fine linen, and goats' hair; ram skins dyed red, badger skins, and acacia wood; oil for the light, and spices for the anointing oil and for the sweet incense; onyx stones, and stones to be set in the ephod and in the breastplate. And let them make Me a sanctuary, that I may dwell among them. According to all that I show you, that is, the pattern of the tabernacle and the pattern of all its furnishings, just so you shall make it."

Where do you think they got this stuff from? Yes, it was the plunder of Egypt. They had absolutely everything they needed for the assignment! God was now requiring them to bring some of it to take care of His kingdom purpose of building a tabernacle. If we wait for instructions after we have acquired our inheritance, we will accomplish the purposes and plans of our Father's heart AND eat the good of the land.

SEED #6

THE GREAT WEALTH TRANSFER – MAKE THE EXCHANGE

I was drifting off to sleep one evening and the Lord said, "You are about to experience the greatest wealth transfer you've ever seen!" I had no idea of how this was going to happen. I have several businesses I am involved in, but I didn't assume that would be the avenue He would take. A week later, again, it was late one evening and I logged into one of my business accounts, to make a gold purchase for my portfolio. When I decided the amount, I moved forward to click the mouse button to make the transfer, and the Holy Spirit said to me VERY clearly, *"Wealth Transfer!"* In a matter of a moment, revelation came crashing in, wave after wave! I got it! My understanding was opened, and I realized this was one of the keys, and a major one, to how this wealth transfer is going to take place. **One of the major ways is through**

<u>the gold market, because gold is real money!</u> An explosion happened in my spirit, and I knew I was pregnant with this revelation that the Holy Spirit wanted released to His people right away. I shared a portion of this information with a business partner, and he said, "You know I have to share this! I have never heard this in my life!" I didn't care, but I know a part of the revelation doesn't do anyone any good other than getting them really excited. Therefore, we don't attain to the fulness of what God has prepared for us, because people get drunk on revelation, or being the first to release something, but they don't get ALL the chapters in the book. As a result, those they release it to will come up short. However, this book is written with **BALANCE** in mind. There are laws that can't be ignored in order for this wealth transfer to be measurable, lasting and sustainable, for generations to come. The second half of this book touches on a few.

At this point I pray the Holy Spirit has opened the eyes of your understanding to the truth concerning money and this wealth transfer. Beloved, gold is money. Gold is one of and a very important aspect of acquiring true wealth. <u>Gold is from God! He made it; now He is raising up kingdom minded people who will heed His voice to go in and redeem this aspect</u>

of His wealth – your inheritance! **The totality of the wealth transfer can't be accomplished without GOLD, make no mistake about it!**

THE RIGHT EXCHANGE

For as long as I can remember, the body of Christ has had its eyes set on the movement of paper money from one group to another, as the means in which this transfer would take place. We've just figured it would change hands. Paper money has lost, is losing and will continue to lose its value, because the standard of gold, God's standard that used to back it, has been removed. As a result, we have found ourselves working harder and harder for a deteriorating "asset." That's why today's income can't purchase anything close to what you could purchase years ago. At some point in our history, there will be a one world currency and it will not be defined by the U.S. The debt we hold with China is an indicator of a real possibility of their nation redefining money as we know it!

How do we move forward to redeem or recover our inheritance with the current revelation we possess? How will we apply this portion of the wealth transfer and use this knowledge to operate in a society which is run by paper money? Let me give you a natural example first and then we will pull back the covers of the delusion, pack our bags and begin our EXODUS out of Egypt, into our promised land. It's our time!

In the currency exchange market, different types of paper money are exchanged, with the hope of profit. There is an inherent risk involved for the reward; Of course, some of that risk can be removed with education and training. One thing, and really the only thing I want to point out about this system, is the fact that different countries exchange currencies for profit. If that's the case in the world system with worldly currency, then where does that leave kingdom people? Isn't there, in fact, a currency we are supposed to be exchanging for? Isn't there a right exchange? Surely, if this world has an exchange system, then the kingdom of God must have one too! One thing I have learned about the systems of the world: they are always a counterfeit of kingdom systems. But we should know how to use the world's form of exchange to procure/redeem REAL wealth!

HOW WILL THIS BE DONE?

A portion of the money seed we gain through our jobs or businesses should be converted to gold. This is no different than making a deposit in your bank account, except your bank account is only a place to store your seed, where those in the world system use it for their own gain. They loan out your money to bring them profit and you get absolutely nothing for it! Yes, you've been helping those in the world's system get rich with your SEED! Now, you must learn how to make the **right exchange**, by exchanging money seed for gold. Our kingdom exchange system is the REAL exchange!

Just a side note, people claim God paves the streets of Heaven with gold because it is of no value. That is so far from the truth! Gold is a STANDARD! Can you imagine your God allowing anything valueless in the realm where He lives? No way! We even saw in the book of Genesis where God called the gold, good. Gold is the red carpet of Heaven and we get to walk on it like the King's kids we profess to be!

Wherever God has positioned you to get your money seed in this hour is irrelevant; but what you do with it will be the deciding factor. Will you be like those in the days of Noah who ignore the warning and drown, or will you survive, as the remnant, because you will decide to come into the ark of safety? This exchange will put you in and keep you in the ark of safety. After the flood is over, we will have further instructions on the conversion of what we have stored up.

SEED #7

THE GREAT WEALTH TRANSFER IN ACTION

In Genesis chapter forty-one, Pharaoh had a dream in which no one could interpret, except Joseph. Through the Spirit of God, Joseph was able to make known the impending economic collapse that was about to level the nation. Joseph didn't hide the revelation from Pharaoh and request a promotion in exchange for the interpretation. No, he cared about the greater good of the people. He cared about the generations to come; therefore, he shared the strategy with Pharaoh immediately.

Then Joseph said to Pharaoh, "The dreams of Pharaoh are one; God has shown Pharaoh what He is about to do: "The seven good cows are seven years, and the seven good heads are seven years; the dreams are one. "And the seven thin and ugly cows which came up after them are seven years, and the seven empty heads blighted by the east wind are seven years of famine. "This is the thing which I have spoken to Pharaoh. God has shown Pharaoh what He is about to do. "Indeed seven years of great plenty will come throughout all the land of Egypt; "but after them seven years of famine will a arise, and all the plenty will be forgotten in the land of Egypt; and the famine will deplete the land. "So the plenty will not be known in the land because of the famine following, for it will be very severe. "And the dream was repeated to Pharaoh twice because the thing is established by God, and God will shortly bring it to pass. "Now therefore, let Pharaoh select a discerning and wise man, and set him over the land of Egypt. "Let Pharaoh do this, and let him appoint officers over the land, **to collect one-fifth of the produce of the land of Egypt in the seven plentiful years. "And let them** <u>GATHER</u> **all the food of those good years that are coming, and store up grain under the authority of Pharaoh, and let them keep food in the cities.** **"Then that food shall be as a reserve for the land for the seven years of famine which shall be in the**

land of Egypt, that the land may not perish during the famine."

Genesis 41:25-36

As you read through the text, you will find that Pharaoh relinquished all authority to Joseph to govern the land and carry out this God ordained strategy to preserve the people. Nothing moved without his word going forth! Oh! that's power! Beloved, God is extending that same grace to the body of Christ in this hour. I want to remind you again; this will be unlike anything we have ever seen. If you look through your Bible, you will find out that the greatest wealth transfers happened during times of famine!

Joseph stored up so much seed, he could no longer keep a record of it. Well that almost seems like hoarding doesn't it? It would, but Joseph had a divine mandate from God to store up for seven years. These were the most prosperous years they had ever seen. As a result, they were able to store up enough to carry nations through the famine for seven years. It may have been tempting to stop gathering because they had plenty, but Joseph was a man who obeyed God. As the famine moved across the land, other nations began to come to Egypt to make an **exchange**. When they ran out of money (silver), they traded their land, property, herds and flocks, their servants, and eventually themselves as slaves.

So, when the money failed in the land of Egypt and in the land of Canaan, all the Egyptians came to Joseph and said, "Give us bread, for why should we die in your presence? For the money has failed." Then Joseph said, "Give your livestock, and I will give you bread for your livestock, if the money is gone." So they brought their livestock to Joseph, and Joseph gave them bread in exchange for the horses, the flocks, the cattle of the herds, and for the donkeys. Thus he fed them with bread in exchange for all their livestock that year. When that year had ended, they came to him the next year and said to him, "We will not hide from my lord that our money is gone; my lord also has our herds of livestock. There is nothing left in the sight of my lord but our bodies and our lands. Why should we die before your eyes, both we and our land? Buy us and our land for bread, and we and our land will be servants of Pharaoh; give us seed, that we may live and not die, that the land may not be desolate." Then Joseph bought all the land of Egypt for Pharaoh; for every man of the Egyptians sold his field, because the famine was severe upon them. So the land became Pharaoh's. And as for the people, he moved them into the cities, from one end of the borders of Egypt to the other end.

Genesis 49:15-21

They brought Joseph the **WEALTH** for the seed. Do you see the culmination and outcome of this wealth transfer? The grain was just like GOLD! They got the SEED and Joseph procured the wealth of the nations! We are in fact doing the opposite. Taking the seed and procuring the gold and storing it up. When the Holy Spirit uncovered this revelation, it kept me up for many nights! Please take note of the sentence I underlined above, **"when the money failed."** The system is going to fail, but those who have prepared will have and be the answer. This is what our wealth transfer looks like!

This transfer requires that we take a portion of our money seed and exchange it for real money— gold, until our storehouse is bursting. This process should continue until God gives us further instruction or another Kairos moment where some of our gold should be brought back into the world system and converted, or the gold itself used for purchases, depending upon what things will look like at the time. Right now, retailers are setting themselves up for the use of gold for everyday purchases! Atm's are being set up for gold exchange. I know this, He who has the gold wins! This next window of opportunity will give us incredible buying power, if we will follow and wait for the instruction. The body of Christ will be the answer to a fledging economy. Like Joseph, we will have the answer. We will have stored up our gold and when it's time for the exchange, we will gain the land, cattle, servants, businesses, and houses. The world will be begging us to take their stuff off their hands, because we will have the gold. Their system will literally work against them, the same way it has worked against us for years.

God is raising up financial deliverers for households and nations right now and I am one of them. What about you? Please know this, there is no generational wealth in paper money! The gold, silver, precious gems, houses, cattle and land are wealth to God. What He created belongs to Him. What belongs to Caesar is Caesar's. What belongs to God is ours!

SEED #8

THE SWITCH IS HERE!

There is an evil I have seen under the sun, As an error proceeding from the ruler: Folly is set in great dignity, While the rich sit in a lowly place. I have seen servants on horses, While princes walk on the ground like servants.

Ecclesiastes 10:5-7

I heard an incredible man of God bring revelation to this Scripture over fifteen years ago and it totally blessed my life! From time to time it continues to come to mind, but as of late, it has been on the forefront of my mind ever since the Lord told me a switch is occurring.

Solomon calls the above scenario, "an evil." What is the evil? The evil is the position of the prince as compared to that of the servant. You and I both know that a prince should never be walking while their servant is riding on the horse. But this WAS the current state of the body of Christ! As sons of God, we have been on foot and in the wrong position for far too long. The sons of the kingdom of darkness have been riding our horses, and it's time for the SWITCH. This switch involves us taking our rightful place as the head, and not the tail. This switch of position can only come as we permit the Holy Spirit to enlarge our capacity, through revelation in His word and by our obedience to what we hear. We were walking because they knew more about our principles than we did! Not only did they know more, but they were putting them to work. They know what the real wealth is, so we had been forced off of our horse.

The switch involves a sudden movement, not just a shifting, put literally a plucking out of one and the putting of another in his/her place. It very much reminds me of a chess game. In the game of chess, the board is surveyed, the positions of the pieces and movement is weighed heavily. You literally play ahead before you move the pieces, to calculate the move of your opponent. Before you know it, you realize that you can strategically move a few pieces and end up with a checkmate! In a moment the opponent realizes a switch is about to occur, and many times there's nothing they can do about it. This is what is happening in the body of Christ this very moment! There is a sudden switch being made which will leave the enemies of God confounded. God has strategically positioned His remnant, those who have ears to hear and have the faith capacity to carry out His plan, to take their place on their horse. The servants won't even see it coming, because it will be so sudden and there's nothing they can do about it! If this is you, I want you to boldly declare, "My switch is here!" You have been walking long enough child of God, it's time to take your place on your horse!

SEED #9

MY ARK OF SAFETY —A GOLDEN OPPORTUNITY

Before I briefly share this golden opportunity, let me say this:

If I have written this book for any purpose other than to warn you of the impending economic flood and the strategy God has outlined for us, may every curse in the book of Deuteronomy twenty-eight come upon me and my household! But, if I have written this book and this chapter with purity of heart and under the influence and direction of the Holy Spirit, may every blessing therein come upon us, for fourteen generations!

As I mentioned, our ark of safety in this hour is gold. GOLD IS MONEY!

The Lord led me to an ark of safety several months ago. My uncovering of it was divine and when I investigated it, the Spirit of the Lord came upon me in a way I have never experienced. It's an incredible business opportunity for those who are looking for one, as well as a means to exchange paper money for gold, for those who just want to protect their families. Through this ark, I have built a very successful business and I am procuring gold and lots of it. I will continue doing so until the Lord gives me further instruction. It would be a horrible thing for me and my family to have found an ark of safety and keep it to ourselves. Therefore, I would like to give you a private invitation. I will stress, this is not the only way to procure gold, but it's the ark of safety the Lord has sent me to. Whatever avenue you choose to make the exchange of paper money to gold, I wish you the best!

May our amazing Father of Lights bless you exceedingly abundantly above all that you can ask or think, according to the power that works in you! I will see you on the other side of **The Great Wealth Transfer!**

<u>www.savegoldmakemoney.com</u>

Questions? Email:
peoplehelping2019@gmail.com

PART II
FOUNDATIONS

PILLAR - 1
FAITH THE FOUNDATION

For the last few years, the Lord has had me shoring up, laying and relaying biblical foundations. Faith was the very first foundation I was assigned. At the onset of the study, I thought I would spend a month or two on the subject, and there I was nine months later still unwrapping this incredible gift of faith. Just recently the Lord shifted my assignment, indicating we needed to move on to a greater glory. He said, "Those who had ears to hear have heard and those who didn't will be left without." God has moved on to something else. The something else is in your hands. He is interested in starting a financial revolution which leads to a financial revival and He can only do this with people whose faith muscle has been developed. He gave us three years to get this area strengthened and now we are to use these hands of faith to grab ahold of our inheritance. This assignment can't be accomplished with feeble hands of faith. Feeble hands are still trying to use faith for cars, houses, rent money, light bills and the necessities of life. They are the very things that our Father knows we have need of! One evening while driving home, the Holy Spirit said, "Too many are spending their faith in the wrong places." Faith was designed to make an exchange between Heaven and earth, to establish the kingdom of God, to be the governor of our lives. Faith is meant to move mountains, to bring forth signs, wonders and miracles, to create. Faith is about doing great exploits and is a benchmark that people who are indoctrinated with kingdom culture exhibit and live by. This pillar is essential to your wealth transfer.

The Bible says in the book of Hebrews 11:6,

But without faith it is impossible to please Him, for he who comes to God must believe that He is, and that He is a rewarder of those who diligently seek Him.

We can't even please God without knowing how to properly live, move and have our being in faith. If you operate in *unwavering* faith it means you are fully persuaded by the Word of God and will not be moved from your position by any person or circumstance.

Faith says, God said it and that settles it. You can visit my podcast for more in-depth teachings on faith **http://www.voiceofreasonpodcast.com**.

Beloved, you will need strong hands of faith in the years to come. Your faith will be on the line; It will be tested to see if it's genuine. Your faith will be exposed for what it is. The last recession which crippled this nation, lasted from December 2007 until June 2009. What is to come will be far greater. During the time when our country was in a recession, there was even talk about a double recession! Great faith, unwavering faith, is not be moved by small talk. I made a statement one time, "I never even participated in the first recession!" Two-thousand seven to Two-thousand nine were at that time, the best financial years of my life! You and I are not part of the world's economy; we operate in the kingdom economy, according to kingdom principles. We DO NOT have to participate in any type of recession, because we are in this world but not of it. Our kingdom economy is failure proof!

Do you recall in the book of Exodus when the Lord released the plagues in the land of Egypt? One thing I remember which fascinated me, is those plagues affected the Egyptians but the Israelites, who were in the land of Goshen were untouchable. Likewise, the perils of this world system's economy have absolutely no power over you when you are in your financial Goshen. You will only look on the plight of the wicked, but it will not come near your dwelling; that is **IF** you have the God kind of faith.

By the way, you can't force the hand of faith. People who try to force faith go from frustration to frustration, instead of from glory to glory! Faith is intended to work in conjunction with the Word, will and the timing of God. The writing of this book and the new assignment I am embarking on was revealed to me seventeen years ago. I came into agreement with the Holy Spirit and I just kept on declaring, walking and moving with Him, knowing at the set time I would have a head on head collision with the Word of God. I didn't have the full picture; I just had a word and that was enough for me. My heart was fixed, trusting in Him. When we truly have a foundation of faith, we will find our faith on our path of obedience. Jesus told the disciples in **John 14:3,**

"And if I go and prepare a place for you, I will come again and receive you to Myself; that where I am, there you may be also."

He was speaking of preparing a place for them in the body of Christ. There is also a concept here the Lord revealed to me five years ago. Where the Word is sent to, you will be there also. So, if I come into agreement with God, speak His word (send it into my future), and operate in faith, where He is, where His Word is, I will find myself right there at the set time. His Word will be right there waiting to escort me into my future! Now, that my friend is faith!

PILLAR - 2

SPEAK THE FATHER'S LANGUAGE

Every culture has a language which quickly identifies what country they are connected to. Those who have been translated into the kingdom of God also have a language which is specific to the culture. Our language is designed to shape our world and bring the regions around us into alignment with our words. The key is this: our words must be His words. His Word is the only language He responds to. Have you ever encountered someone who speaks a foreign language and needs help? You desperately want to understand them. You try hard to make out what they are saying, to no avail. Because you don't understand their language, you are unable to move on their behalf. Therefore, their situation goes unresolved. Do you know this is the same frustration our Father and heavenly angels deal with? The angels of the Lord do not harken to the voice of tears or frustration. They only harken to the one who puts a voice to His Word, as evidenced in **Psalm 103:20:**

Bless the Lord, you His angels, Who excel in strength, who do His word, Heeding the voice of His word.

I have a question for you; are you speaking the Father's language over your finances, or do your words agree with your present circumstances? Are you speaking words of lack, limitation, not enough, just enough, or never enough? Regardless of where you find yourself financially, one of the pillars which must always be in place, is speaking the WORD only. Anything other than that is a foreign language to the Father which is unenforceable by the Holy Spirit and your ministering angels! Don't expect God to respond when you're babbling. This is one of the reasons why the body of Christ does not see manifestation of the Word of God in the area of our finances; We're speaking a foreign language and expect a God **interpreted** manifestation. This will never happen.

Look at what God said in Jeremiah,

> *Moreover the word of the Lord came to me, saying, "Jeremiah, what do you see?" And I said, "I see a branch of an almond tree." Then*

the Lord said to me, "You have seen well, for I am ready to perform My word."

Jeremiah 1:11-12

Either we speak His word and speak it consistently or we will continue to go wanting. It's so easy to cast the blame for our lack on God, on the economy, or our boss; but He said, He watches over His Word to perform it. If we don't give Him anything to perform, there's only one person to blame. Your money, lack of or abundance of, starts in your mouth! Abundance will only manifest when your words are an echo of what the Holy Spirit is saying. The last time I heard a voice echo, it sounded the same from release to finish. You can't start with the Word and finish with a foreign language!

He is READY to perform His word; Are you ready to release it? If you desire to see life breathed into your financial situation, begin planting the Word in your heart and speaking/declaring the Word over your financial future every day. It doesn't matter what your financial situation is right now. When the medicine of the Word of God is applied to that cancerous financial condition, it must change!

> *"Brood of vipers! How can you, being evil, speak good things? For out of the abundance of the heart the mouth speaks"*
>
> *Matthew 12:34*

The mouth speaks from the abundance of the heart! Whatever you are speaking today about your finances is a result of what you have stored up in your heart. In this case the heart He is talking about is your soul, which is your mind, emotions and your will. Whatever you have focused on is now coming out of your mouth. What do you think would happen to your financial situation if you stopped meditating on not having enough or barely getting by, and filled your mind with the Word of God? Speak it AND let it get in you and restructure your financial DNA, so the characteristics of your economy begin to change. You would find yourself experiencing the life He promised you.

Allow a new language to be planted in your spirit. **Isaiah 55:11** says the **"Word of God can't return void."** Once it's released with faith and revelation, it must come back with the package. *Luke 21:33* says Heaven and earth will pass away, but His words will never pass away. **Psalm 119:89** says the Word is forever settled in heaven. When you speak the Father's language in faith, His Word must produce.

PILLAR - 3
USE WHAT YOU GOT!

T here is a prevailing unspoken truth in the body of Christ, that he who can quote the most Scriptures has the most power. The quoting of Scripture sounds beautiful and powerful, but if there is no demonstration, this display has the same effect of a child memorizing and repeating words for a spelling test. We were never told to be merely memorizers of the Word, but doers of it. You would not believe how many in the body of Christ are stuck simply because they are not doers of the word.

> *But be doers of the word, and not hearers only, deceiving yourselves. For if anyone is a hearer of the word and not a doer, he is like a man observing his natural face in a mirror; for he observes himself, goes away, and immediately forgets what kind of man he was. But he who looks into the perfect law of liberty and continues in it, and is not a forgetful hearer*

but a doer of the work, this one will be blessed in what he does.

James 1: 22-25

James makes it very clear; we must be DOERS of the Word of God. Listening to and quoting Scriptures on financial prosperity will not make you rich any more than listening to and quoting medical terms will make you a doctor. There are steps and processes which must be put in place if you want to become a doctor. We apply doing in other areas of life almost effortlessly and neglect it in our financial lives.

Early in my Christian walk, I found myself crying out to the Lord for financial relief. It seemed everything in my life had been intentionally turned upside down; but my financial state was the most pressing, to me, at the time. One day as I was reading my Word, I landed in Exodus chapter fourteen

And the Lord said to Moses, "Why do you cry to Me? Tell the children of Israel to go forward. But lift up your rod, and stretch out your hand over the sea and divide it. And the children of Israel shall go on dry ground through the midst of the sea."

Exodus 14:15-16

As soon as I saw the text, it became alive in me, and the Holy Spirit spoke very clearly to me and asked me a question that changed the entire course of my life, *"Why do you keep calling out to me to do what I have already equipped you to do?"* Oh, I got it in an instant! We spend so much time talking about what God is going to do just like Moses was doing. It sounds great, but there's no power in that. You can't stand at the Red Sea of life and talk about what God is going to do, especially when you've had the training needed to complete the work.

God has set something in your hand and its mighty when He is permitted to get in it, the same way He was in Moses' rod. Our financial seed gives Him access to our financial economy. Instead of sowing, and working the principles of increase, many believers stand at their Red Sea and cry out to God, who will never show up because He has already given them the rod and the training to go across on dry ground. He's saying the same thing to you in which He said to Moses, **"Why are you crying out to me, stretch out your rod!"** It's time for you to use what He has placed in your hands. It's time to sow in faith. It's time to believe and apply the Word of God to your finances.

There is also instruction which can only come from the Holy Spirit. We call this a rhema word. He is known as the teacher of profit and has insight into the treasures of darkness and hidden riches in secret places. These hidden riches are more than just tangible assets; Revelation is as much of a tangible asset as any other tangible good.

> *I will give you the treasures of darkness and hidden riches of secret places, That you may know that I, the LORD, Who call you by your name, Am the God of Israel (Isaiah 45:3-5).*

It's easy to throw our financial situation back on God; but beloved, He has already given us a life manual, a starter faith pack and seed. What we do with it is up to us! It is definitely time to use what you got!

PILLAR - 4
THE TITHE AND THE OFFERING

Surely you didn't think I would overlook this important pillar. It must be addressed because the tithe continues to be one of the most controversial subjects in the church today. Failure to execute, as well as the lack of revelation in this area is a roadblock for many. Many take the escape hatch of it being Old Testament doctrine. I encourage you to read the Word for yourself and allow the Holy Spirit to reveal the truth of this pillar. You may also get a copy of my Book, *"Break Out of Poverty Into Financial Abundance."* There is also a great mini book by Dr. Tom Leding entitled *"Tithing Is Not Optional."* If you're not tithing consistently and in faith, you are not ready for this wealth transfer. If you are not tithing, I can guarantee the devourer, Satan, is having a field-day with your finances, health, marriage or the lives of your children. Until you grasp the relevance and power of the tithe, it's impossible to walk into your wealthy place.

> *"Bring all the tithes into the storehouse, that there may be food in My house, And try Me now in this," Says the LORD of hosts, "If I will not open for you the windows of heaven And pour out for you such blessing that there will not be room enough to receive it."*
>
> *Malachi 3:10*

The tithe is ten percent of your gross income. For example, if you make $500 per week before deductions, then $50 would be the amount of your tithe. We don't throw God our leftovers after we have deducted our savings, health insurance, life insurance, and paid our bills and say, "Here's your tithe!" That's called tipping, not tithing. It's also called stealing because the tithe belongs to Him! In Malachi chapter one, God told the priests they had been treating Him irreverently as a Father. He then advises them how to return to Him and treat Him accordingly, by bringing the whole tithe into the storehouse. When you tithe, you return what already belongs to Him! So, you haven't even begun giving until the tithe is returned. Your Father put the tithe in place, to ensure you know who your source is, for the protection of your economy, as a means for you to honor Him as the King, and to walk in the fullness of His blessing.

THE POWER OF THE OFFERING

Let's look at Malachi chapter three again for a moment, but this time let's look at verse eight.

"Will a man rob God? Yet you have robbed Me! But you say, 'In what way have we robbed You?' In tithes and offerings."

My friend, it's more than just a dime on every dollar; God expects an offering as well! To be honest with you, God expects full access to ALL your resources. An offering given by someone who does not tithe and vice versa, ensures the devourer will be waiting with an outstretched hand to consume whatever return comes in. It will appear that something is always breaking down, or some situation arises which always costs you some MONEY! This is the job of the devourer and he is very good at it. If you will obey the Word, God promises to rebuke the devourer, or stop the hand of Satan from devouring your harvest and bless you beyond measure. The offering and seed are what brings increase in your life. The tithe sets the stage, but the offering and seed allows financial blessing to flow. If you don't tithe and give offerings, it's very unlikely that your store of money seed will increase.

When you refuse to return the tithe and give a free-will offering, you ROB God! Nobody likes to use this word in the pulpit anymore. We want to talk about all the blessing, but don't want to bring correction and accountability to those who are stealing from the Father. I believe God's question was one of mere amazement, astonishment and perplexity. Will a man really try to defraud and despoil God? Yes, it's happening every day in the body of Christ. I personally believe a person must be out of their mind to steal from God. I tried it once when my son was two years old and I never did it again!

Look at what happens when you give in the kingdom:

> *Give, and it will be given to you: good measure, pressed down, shaken together, and running over will be put into your bosom. For with the same measure that you use, it will be measured back to you.*
>
> *Luke 6:38*

In the Scripture above we see what's called, the Law of Reciprocity. It means whatever is given will come back in a greater measure. This applies to your financial seed as well. Your one act of giving releases a violent outpouring of the Father's blessing on your behalf; and it comes through men. The end of the verse says the measure you use will be measured back to you. You are the one who decides how you want to receive. If you want to receive abundance, then you must break your $1, $5, $10 giving limits and allow the Holy Spirit to instruct you on the amount to give. There is nothing more powerful than a financial seed sown in the amount and place the Holy Spirit directs!

PILLAR - 5
HONOR

Honor is a pillar which somehow has gotten lost in the body of Christ. One of the reasons there is such a hard time with this one is because we have become too buddy buddy with those in authority over our lives. We want a friend more than we want a spiritual father. We want someone to tickle our ears and make us feel good more than we want a man or woman of God to correct and direct us. We have become too familiar with our spouses and wonder why we are not seeing results from tithing and sowing. Wives are trying to lead the household instead of the husband. How in the world can you honor anyone you don't even respect? How do you honor, when you don't submit to those in authority?

In Scripture, the men/women of God had a place of prominence and respect with the people. They understood the cost if they spoke harshly against them. One account of this principle, which I have always kept before me is found in the book of Numbers. This refers to all categories mentioned above. Even if a pastor dishonors those in his congregation or his spouse, he will have to answer to God. Dishonor is unacceptable on every level.

Then Miriam and Aaron spoke against Moses because of the Ethiopian woman whom he had married; for he had married an Ethiopian woman. So they said, "Has the Lord indeed spoken only through Moses? Has He not spoken through us also?" And the Lord heard it. (Now the man Moses was very humble, more than all men who were on the face of the earth.) Suddenly the Lord said to Moses, Aaron, and Miriam, "Come out, you three, to the tabernacle of meeting!" So the three came out. Then the Lord came down in the pillar of cloud and stood in the door of the tabernacle, and called Aaron and Miriam. And they both went forward. Then He said, "Hear now My words: If there is a prophet among you, I, the Lord, make Myself known to him in a vision; I speak to him in a dream. Not so with My servant Moses; He is faithful in all My house. I speak with him face to face,

Even plainly, and not in dark sayings; And he sees the form of the Lord. Why then were you not afraid To speak against My servant Moses?" So the anger of the Lord was aroused against them, and He departed. And when the cloud departed from above the tabernacle, suddenly Miriam became leprous, as white as snow. Then Aaron turned toward Miriam, and there she was, a leper.

Numbers 12:1-10

Your position under those in authority is your place of protection, sustainment and provision; that's why God placed you there. When you begin to dishonor or disrespect him or her, you will suffer, yes even financially. I have seen this happen repeatedly. Not only have I seen it, but have personally experienced it. I became offended by a very prominent tv minister whom I was partnered with and began to say some things I shouldn't have. I disconnected from the ministry. After a short period of time, I began to suffer financially. One day, the Holy Spirit gently spoke to me about what I had done and urged me to repent. I wrote the pastor a letter asking him for his forgiveness, even though he knew nothing of what I had said.

He who receives a prophet in the name of a prophet shall receive a prophet's reward. And he who receives a righteous man in the name of a righteous man shall receive a righteous man's reward.

Matthew 10:41

How you receive the man or woman of God determines the reward you are able to withdraw from their anointing. How you receive your spouse determines your reward.

HOW DO WE HONOR?

Honor involves more than just lip service. If you truly honor the man or woman of God in your life, then you should also have no problem blessing them financially, whether they take a salary or are wealthy or not. We are so quick to tell our leaders how much we love him or her. We expect them to be available all hours at our beckon call, but let someone mention giving them a raise or giving them a financial gift, then the real heart of the person is revealed. Love gives. Your Heavenly Father gave His Son as a demonstration of His love for you. I believe we need to get back to honoring the men and women of God by words and by blessing them financially.

Honor is important to God. We can't say we honor God but dishonor those around us. Your destiny is locked up in a man or woman of God. Your destiny is in your spouse. After God, they are the first place to set your honor. Don't you dare honor others more than you do them! I taught a lesson many years ago entitled, "Honor Gets the Blessing." Not only did I teach it, but it's a standard I try to live by. This pillar can't be ignored in the great wealth transfer.

PILLAR - 6
LOVE

You're probably wondering why this chapter would be included in a book about the kingdom wealth transfer. The Lord asked me to add this chapter because He wants you to know how very important love is with this assignment. There is no force greater than the love of God. Our display of love is proof that we are His disciples and love Him. Don't talk to me about loving Jesus whom you can't see, and you refuse to walk in love with the brethren whom you can see!

This wealth transfer will happen with or without your participation, but if you are in fact accepting the invitation, please know your posture toward those in the world must be love.

"A new commandment I give to you, that you love one another; as I have loved you, that you also love one another. By this all will

know that you are My disciples, if you have love for one another."

John 13:34-35

Power and money magnify or exposes the character of people. If you really want to know the heart of those close you, give them some money or power. You will see pride and arrogance rear its ugly head, from those who are not grounded in humility. One thing God hates is pride. People who truly walk in and understand the love of God know how vital it is to stay in a posture of humility.

Even though Joseph was held captive in Pharaoh's prison for years, he still treated Pharaoh and the nation of Egypt with love. This was evidenced in his willingness to reveal God's plan to save the nations. Joseph did not ask for anything in return from a system that had him bound for most of his youth! The love of God unveiled the dream and its remedy, and that same love put a system in place to preserve the wicked and the just. This must be the same posture we walk in during and after this wealth transfer is complete.

God is strategically moving His people into places of influence even as I write this book. Therefore, it's vital that we remember to treat those of this world with the love of the Father as we take positions of influence. It's important we remember where the Lord has brought us from and how He has forgiven us of so much. Because we have been forgiven much, I believe if anybody should know how to walk in love, it should be God's people! A wealth transfer without love isn't a wealth transfer at all.

CONCLUSION

If you've taken time to read this book through the Holy Spirit, you should feel a stirring in your spirit right now. You should sense the overthrowing of your current financial government. You should be declaring, "I want my REAL money, wealth and riches right now!" You should have realized a revolution has begun! Beloved, I want to encourage you to take time to go back through this manual several times and read some of the other books I have referenced. You can't permit the urgency of this call to diminish.

Your Father has given you the opportunity, responsibility and privilege of redeeming your inheritance. This is **YOUR** exodus; what will you do from here? I pray you will take heed to what is written herein and get yourself, your family and those close to you, to an ark of safety. You MUST have gold in the hour to come and you MUST be proficient in faith and biblical financial principles, or you will not endure the coming economic deluge.

May our Lord richly reward you for your obedience as you continue in these *Seeds of Prosperity For a Financial Revolution.* I decree and declare your outcome and that of your household, is an AWAKENING which leads to financial REVIVAL as you embark on a journey leading to the greatest wealth transfer the body of Christ has ever seen!

ABOUT THE AUTHOR

Apostle Sonya L. Thompson of ARISE Ministries International is called as a teacher to the body of Christ to; **"Train, Educate and Advise through the Gospel with Simplicity and Purity."** She holds a Bachelor of Science in the field of Business Administration, a Master of Arts in Biblical Leadership and a Doctorate in Biblical Finances. She is an entrepreneur, mentor and spiritual mother. Apostle Thompson was ordained as a Pastor by world renowned minister of the gospel, Dr. Nasir Siddiki and affirmed as an Apostle by Apostle Jerry D. Owens of Joshua Generation Outreach Church; He is her Pastor & covering of the **ARISE Apostolic Network** & **ARISE Ministries International.**

She is driven to introduce people to the Living God; To teach the Living word; To equip & edify the body of Christ for the work of ministry; To lead others to encounter the abiding presence of God in a way which will forever change their lives; To see an **Awakening** that leads to **Revival**!

Other Books By Dr. Sonya L. Thompson

Business By The Bible

Seeds of Prosperity

Break Out of Poverty Into Financial Abundance

Declare Yourself Wealthy

Glory Walkers Revealed

Fully Functional Faith Series

He Restores My Soul

All books available on amazon or visit

www.ariseministriesintl.com

To book Dr. Thompson send booking requests

to: Info@ariseministriesintl.com